HECTOR

At Ground Level
and Beyond

Having searched most of my life for the illusive "Philosopher's Stone," I enjoyed reading and reflecting about the journey of Hector. A delightfully entertaining and thought-provoking story, Hector reminds us that our search for the horizon can blind us to the treasures at our feet and that our true home will always be found precisely where our hearts are.

Tom Mitchell Ph.D

Hector At Ground Level cuts to the core of heart and soul, awakening us to what is vastly most important as we navigate these precious lives of ours. With love at its center, the words dance off the page and into our senses and are a delight for the child in all of us, while gently and safely prodding our adult to take a deep breath into this moment with all the fullness we can muster. Filled with the depth of inspiration, the poetry of life shines throughout the book and leaves the reader with a feeling of possibility, joy and love, and a reminder that it all begins at home, right here, inside each of us.

Carol Goldberg

Hector At Ground Level is a beautiful, lyrical, modern-day fable starring one very introspective hedgehog. It is a love letter to love, and an invitation for readers to consider their choices in life. Through elegant prose and beautiful imagery, Finnan reminds us to be present in our everyday lives. A treasure!

Windy Lynn Harris - Author

Hector At Ground Level, a Very Simple Love Story, by Gary Finnan, is a fable in the tradition of Winnie the Pooh or Jonathan Livingston Seagull. Hector, an introspective hedgehog, is a middle-aged male with grown children and a loving wife (Hillary). Yet, he's quite dissatisfied with what seems to him a mediocre existence. As he mulls over his life, working for years at the slug farm, he finds himself depressed and melancholy.

Some of the writing in this sweet story is beautifully poetic, some is a flowing stream-of-consciousness, yet all of it invites readers to consider their own lives and the choices they make that either enrich or enervate. Although this is a small book, it deals with significant themes, and it deals with them tenderly. It's a book I'll read more than once.

Sunny Lockwood

Hector At Ground Level is a beautifully written book that needs to be read and absorbed by everyone living in today's world. Story aside, the writing is soft and soothing; there are many, many phrases and lines to be savored and revisited over time. The author follows Hector, a hedgehog with a comfortable life, as he reflects on the choices he has made over his life. Hector comes to realize that while he, like many of us, has spent much of his life pursuing things that don't bring happiness, happiness has always been there for the taking.

In turns, a parable, and a beautiful love story, *Hector At Ground Level*, lovingly offers readers an opportunity to step back and reflect on what brings true happiness and contentment in our lives. Hector discovers that it's not about living up to the expectations of others or acquiring things or endlessly racing toward a goal that can never be achieved, it's about understanding that each of us is already complete and happiness awaits us at every turn, if we're only willing and able to see and grab it. Highly recommended.

Jim Brumm - Author

I didn't know, at first, about this little paperback book. But, as I delved into it, I realized I was looking into the mirror of my life. Plagued always by indecision, I, like Hector, had to eventually come into my own and make the decision of a lifetime: to allow happiness by recognizing the best in front of me. This book could not have come at a better time.

I love to read tasty books, and this one is delicious. The poetic way that Gary reveals Hector's life is mesmerizing, reminding me of my childhood when I had just discovered the wonder of books. This book is something that you can hold on to and come back to often, at different stages in your life. An excellent gift for anyone at any age, as you read it, you will truly feel like you are drinking a cup of that Chamomile tea Hector enjoys so much.

Every sentence, every line of prose is infused with lovely summertime wonder, and the message becomes clearer as you read: decisions are often difficult, just as life is, but, if you be still and allow it, your answers will come... even if in a dream.

Nanette Stein

My favorite part? "Hector's" ramblings at the end; a glimpse into his essence through his somewhat private poetry about his own journey and love for his little family. These are a savory, soothing, and comforting invitation to reflect upon your own life. So magical and well written, these lines stoked my book-loving taste buds and were the most delicious of them all.

A charming book—what makes this book so unique is the author's excellent use of language. It is simple, but at the same time, precious and poetic. Finnan delivers his gentle philosophy through Hector, a hedgehog. We easily identify with Hector's foibles and doubts. The reader grows with Hector as this loveable creature expands and learns to embrace his family and the wonders of his life. This is a great book to read at night before going to bed. You'll have a wonderful night's sleep as your head hits the pillow feeling "all's right with the world."

Jean Wong

Gary Finnan skillfully delivers serious life lessons told through the eyes of an imaginary hedgehog and his family living in a world with the trappings of humans, but "at ground level." *Hector At Ground Level* is thought-provoking, entertaining, and fulfilling to read. Relatively short, it succinctly makes the point that happiness is often found in the place that we seldom think to look: In our everyday surroundings, relationships, and activities.

Charles Carroll

I have read the book twice and love it and will read it again. It has a very comforting flow to it. I have described it as like a warm blanket. It's a simple story that eloquently describes the cycle of life from youth to middle age. It's the kind of book you take some time with and ponder. The language the author uses is quite beautiful.

Mark Hullinger

Feeling a pleasant warmth, emerging from the world of Hector, I smile. The imagery in this book created a natural world that feels so simple, so right, so parallel with my own life. Thank you, Gary Finnan, for sharing your thoughts in such a delightful way.

Dawn L. Anderson

Hector At Ground Level takes us on a journey of life's emotions through the eyes of a hedgehog. The imagery is amazing, and the words powerful and poetic. I love this book!
Connie Caudill

Gary has told a wonderful story about appreciating what you have. Gratitude is good! The illustrations are adorable. I especially loved the poetry, which was heartfelt and touching.

Sharon M. Stroick, Ph.D., MCIP

Also by Gary Finnan

Billy Tapper Zillionaire

This Book Belongs To

_____

HECTOR

At Ground Level and Beyond

A Very Simple Love Story

Gary Finnan

Wellness Writers Press

WELLNESS WRITERS PRESS
An imprint of Pure Ink Press

Paperback ISBN: 979-8-9876015-1-8
Ebook ISBN: 979-8-9876015-2-5

Art by Camryn Finnan and Elina Cherianidou

First edition by NorlightsPress 2019
Second edition by Wellness Writers Press 2023

wellnesswriterspress.com
www.pureinkpress.com

For my flowers,
Eva, Cam and Mac

FOREWORD

Hector At Ground Level is a courageous and honest modern-day fable of love, disappointment, dreams, and the angst of decision making. The author uses elegant and lyrical prose to tell the magical story of the life and reflections and of an increasingly loving and self-aware hedgehog. We forget these are the words of animal we know nothing about because we quickly understand and recognize their emotions, fears, and excitement.

This fable has much for many readers. It is a love story; it is also a story of values, personal needs, and coming of age. It illustrates the ups and downs of the journey of life in a stark, but true fashion.

The story of brave, but sometimes misguided and angry, Hector brings to mind many of my life coaching and therapy clients. These amazing people are often troubled by choices they made in life and continually second guess themselves. Often, this causes them to be stuck in inertia as they wonder if the grass is greener on the other side. This place is disempowering, because not much change can happen in a place of indecision. The author brings this pain and ambiguity alive in the most heart-warming and insightful manner.

This book is appropriate for both men and women embarking on adult life through midlife, and into their twilight years. In a gentle way, it gives readers permission to explore their own feelings around life purpose and family relationships by understanding their reactions to the hedgehogs' thoughts and interpretation of what has happened in his life. Once self-aware, Hector displays stoic personal responsibility and seeks to acquiesce his ego and support his loved ones so he may also be happier in life.

The book ends peacefully and is followed by a series of honest "Ramblings," a series of poems written by Hector over the years. Seemingly, this is the one way he could express himself without self-judgment and overcome the fear of looking weak in the eyes of others. These poems are touching, beautiful, and thought-provoking—well worth a few reads.

—Priya Rana Kapoor Executive Life Coach, Speaker, and Author of *Give Yourself Permission*

All answers lay brooding beneath that thin veneer of dust
that had settled on his life, a dust that makes great beauty
slightly dull, much the same way a thought perceived
through a gossamer screen of fear obscures a life better
lived, manipulating one's perspective, fueling reality and
discontent at not having enough.

Contents

Life unfolds, day by day, at ground level,
amid brush and scrub.

Prologue – At Once 1

Chapter 1 – At Ten 11

Chapter 2 – At Twenty 19

Chapter 3 – At Thirty 29

Chapter 4 – At Forty 37

Chapter 5 – At Last 49

Chapter 6 – At Fifty 55

Ramblings 61

Epilogue – At Sixty and Beyond 97

Hector: A Reflection of Sorts 133

Author and Artists 159

It's the women in our lives that make men of us.

Mothers, sisters, lovers, wives and daughters.

For a wee kiss from their sweet lips,

makes us simple men, big...

Prologue – At Once

Sitting there, in the dimly lit burrow, Hector drew a breath infused with sweet chamomile tobacco, the smoke pulled slowly through the old clay pipe his grandmother had used as she rocked him to sleep when he was a pup. Hector drew deeply on his pipe and held his breath unconsciously, his calloused paw tightening around the pipe. He considered his life now, and upon reflection, grew agitated and resentful. Finally breathing, he let out a long winding plume of smoke; it curled and twisted, floating up to the roof of the burrow where it hung above him as a dull cloud of pity.

From the darkness and comfort of the overstuffed chair, Hector watched the light and shadows from the fireplace bouncing around the room - flashes of yellow, orange and black, leaping, elusive shapes dancing on the walls, chasing the feelings around his chest, mesmerizing him into a vacant trance.

Rising stiffly from the comfort of the chair, Hector stumbled out of the burrow into the surrounding forest. Instinctively pacing through the darkness, he realized that his life had stalled. Here he was, somewhere between "full steam ahead" and "I give up." It wasn't just his job at the slug farm; it was everything: kids, wife, burrow, friends, and all the "others" that drew upon him.

Exhausted, resigned to silence, he walked; simply savoring the breaking of little twigs and damp leaves underfoot, enjoying the familiar woodland smells. What small compensation, to wander aimlessly in solitude through the night, seeking space to think.

The light of home shone through the trees, a distant sanctuary amid the muddle of thoughts. Disoriented, it took a moment to recognize how far he had walked off the track. Hector questioned the pillar of strength they had told him to be. Who were they to define his life?

Was it all real or a belief? He could run, he could hide, he could survive like this, but he could not live like this he thought. Darkness engulfed him as he walked back to the sanctuary of the burrow.

Once back within the light of the burrow, Hector rummaged through a pile of old books that were stacked on a shelf in the corner of the den. He huffed and hawed, consumed by his own discontent. A pressure built behind his eyes, too much elderberry wine and all the reason in the world to be encumbered by this melancholy.

The scurry of many tiny legs, a millipede, plucked up, quickly eyed, then consumed carelessly, "Where's my damn stuff? She has bloody well cleaned up again," he growled, to no one, as he looked for his book.

Crunching at the remainder of the lifeless morsel, Hector brushed the winter's dust away, sipped the sweet elderberry nectar, and pulled his scarf around himself, shuddering deeply within, trying to ignore his ever-present companion, discontent.

Hector shuffled over to a bookcase and started to pull remnants from the shelves, stirring an eddy of dust. A little book fell and bashed him upon the snout, causing him to jump back with a start, growling between clenched teeth. It had hurt more than he cared for. Consumed with the task of resurrecting his own writings, he had not considered discovering hers.

The little book gazed up from the floor, wrapped in a covering of embossed flowers, scribbling, and doodles. It had been constructed with care, he thought, still retaining an aura of its former beauty, despite being a little faded and worn on the outside. This little book had traveled a journey. Hillary's journey, a life she had before him, a life he had been a part of yet never thought to fully embrace in his haste.

Hector brushed back the gray from his temples, poked his glasses into focus and shuffled back over to the large chair next to the fireplace.

He sat back deep into the chair that was overstuffed with rabbit hair and fine bull rush downy and considered the contents of his discovery. The writing on the cover was hers, Hillary's. The strong rounded, practical lettering finishing with hoops and swirls, little love hearts and crosses he vaguely recognized from a time gone by. He sniffed at the book expecting to catch her scent, but alas, nothing, only dry paper.

Hillary had gone to market in the next village and had been gone three days; she sold early spring posies bright and gay, small woven baskets and sweet honey treats. He had let her go as the birds woke, chirping to the dawn's first light. With a gruff "Goodbye," Hector had kissed her cheek, consumed by the weight of his world and the inconvenience her departure would bring.

We have love, Hector thought to himself. Hillary and I have raised our offspring, we have made a warm burrow and we have built a winter store year after year as necessary for our survival.

Yet, days go by when we neglected to care for each other's burdens, or when we pass each other abruptly in the burrow entrance when I, bringing in fresh grubs for tea, or she, going out to collect the washing from the line miss the chance to reach out and touch one another gently.

That was life...now! How then did we get to this, Hector wondered? Curious now, Hector ran his thumb along the spine and across the tattered bookends, flipping the pages, trying hard not to look inside. Little hearts, different scribbles and pasted notes flashed in a blur, tempting and teasing his curiosity.

We have trust I am sure, he thought. We share the tasks of planning the winter store, trading with the mice and squirrels, helping get the children to school, all the tasks of everyday life.

They had spoken of dreams over the years, he was sure.

Hector had aspired to write "something." He had vented his passion in youth and now in middle age, his discontent on scraps of paper that lived under bottles of elderberry wine.

Hillary, on the other hand, had proclaimed that she, "never thought of such things." At least, she said, "not enough to write them down."

Now, here he sat, colorful little book in hand, randomly gazing at obvious pages, blurting names, times and places, ending in declarations of passion and unrequited love for others in her youth before Hector.

Hector realized he'd allowed Hillary to erode before his eyes, he had allowed time to diminish her very essence, the very thing that drew him to her all those years ago. Her quick wit, her choosing of bright scarves, her love of bold flowers, and her ability to create and believe in the good in every situation or being she encountered.

Hector knew that there had been other loves in her life. How could there not be for one such as she? Hillary must have had suitors enough.

Her grace was in the simple ability to let all who knew her, love her as they drifted on the tide that would ebb and flow in and out of her life. She bestowed effortlessly each friendship with declarations of life lived, explored, and nurtured. Hector felt like an intruder, this access to a guarded place deep in Hillary's past, private remnants of her heart, brief windows of passions held dear.

Paging to the end of the little book, finding his name in that steady flowery hand he knew so well, how strange, he thought, to see it flowing on these weathered pages, gilded with talk of love. Hector felt his heart quicken and shame. How had he forgotten to notice all this in her, the beauty she conveyed so effortlessly in simple words?

Second, to the last page, a napkin tucked between the stained cover fell to the floor, he lifted it gently, unfolding it, and therein read his own ode to their beginning. He looked at his clumsy writing, embarrassed by the roughness of it, amused at the honesty of it.

Youthful and consumed with wonder he had written, remembering the question once posed, "What changed in me, Hillary?" Memories of first love flooded in around him, Hector gasped for air as the distant memory pushed hard against him. Closing the book abruptly with a sense of guilt and regret at his foolishness, Hector had the overwhelming desire to reach out and beg forgiveness, not for reading of her passion or her loves long passed, but for forgetting how to love her as much as she deserved, love he knew she wished for and needed.

Sitting there, Hector struggled to summon the passion that she had seen in him so long ago. Delving deep into his heart, he stood, devoid of any real feeling, only the heavy blanket of regret that hung around him. Wandering the familiar burrow, now restless, the wine wearing thin, a candle in his paw, Hector paused. In the dim light, he gazed at the little spiky balls curled up in the big leafy nest in the corner.

"This has happened to you," he remembered Hillary saying so long ago while munching maggot pies, laughing, and rubbing snouts, holding hands as she cupped her pregnant belly.

Hector knew that everyone loved Hillary for her sweet honesty and natural beauty, they loved her for thinking less of herself and so much more of others, for the passion she put into even the simplest task, for the love and nurturing she gave her children and friends daily.

How had Hector drifted so far away into his self-absorbed world? What was it he sought? What was it he felt he lacked? Slumping wearily back into the chair again, the realization came to him. The pain on his snout from the little book had drifted into his heart, lying there uneasily, all this prompted by the discovery of something of immense beauty and immeasurable value in a corner of a dusty room. Hector sat, not knowing what to do with the knowledge that everything he needed was here, right around him in plain sight.

All answers lay brooding beneath that thin veneer of dust that had settled on his life, a dust that makes great beauty slightly dull, much the same way a thought perceived through a gossamer screen of fear obscures a life better lived, manipulating one's perspective, fueling a false reality and discontent at not having enough.

The rustle of leaves and the scurry of paws in the burrow entrance shook Hector from his thoughts. Springing from the chair, he ran up the tunnel to confront the intruder, primal instincts kicking in. Half-blind and disoriented in the dark, Hector faced the shadow coming down into the burrow. Teeth bared and expecting the worst, his eyes found their focus on the intruder to his domain.

"It's me. I'm home. I missed you," Hillary said in a whisper.

With the softest touching of snouts and a sigh of relief, Hector and Hillary shuffled down the burrow together, holding hands and talking of how fine the sunrise would look.

"Thank you for coming home, my love," Hector said with more honesty than he realized.

Everything half alive screams out from the dust.

Some craving the rain, and food, some needing

cleansing, and so few for the pure joy of it.

The cycle complete, from craving to share, proof

now that all will turn in time...

Chapter 1 – At Ten

Hector dropped from his mother's womb, into the brisk air of the burrow, landing with a start on the rough straw-covered floor. "Number seven" she gasped, too young for so large a first litter.

Six others were already there, squirming with blind eyes, driven by instinct to feed at all costs.

Hector, or #7 for the time being, joined the wriggling pink fray in pursuit of the elusive teat. Life started like this, and one could only assume that it might get better.

Wisdom and general belief claimed that for most, life would improve; it started with struggle and a heavy dose of ignorance. This was life at ground level.

At school and from an early age Hector was never quite able to understand Dick and Jane, The Big Red Ball or the unusual shape of the number 5 amid the mumblings of his teacher, Miss Pettigrew.

Hector's memories of remedial reading, of being "slower" than normal, sat heavy upon him. He knew no better.

"God help the little bugger when we start with sums," he heard them whisper. It all became a blur, albeit a consistent one, struggling to pass a test or just keep up with the rabbits or weasels in class.

It all felt just like running last in a race, never understanding why others could run so fast, so effortlessly, never breaking that tape with a puffed-out chest. Why? Who knows?

He knew no better.

Mediocre was a word he had not yet discovered but was entangled in by circumstance of birth.

Nothing changed over his early years other than the skill to hide the fear, cheat the system, and cheat himself with life's little shortcuts through the brambles. Duck and dive, move, and twist Hector learned. "Push him through," they whispered.

Still, cautiously they countered, "Hedgehogs can turn if provoked, be careful. They can also display considerable charm should they choose to."

Discovery of an above-average histrionic ability came as an epiphany after many falls, thanks to Miss Gail, a fine golden albino ferret, his teacher from the Scottish Highlands. Her gift was promoting Hector from playing a stoic tree at the edge of the stage to a small part with dialogue, and admittance into the chorus of the school play. Hector resolved instinctively that he would simply finish one step at a time and sing along the way.

Hector's parents, Maggie and Drew bestowed upon their brood of seven a fragile birthright amid muddy fields and waterlogged hedgerows.

Drew was what you might call a well-oiled old bastard. He had all the classic traits of a Hedgehog: short stubby legs, the customary prickly exterior when pushed too far, and an underbelly much softer than he would have liked to admit. Drew styled a furry chin and a pair of narrow eyes, constantly on the lookout for a bit of fluff who would listen to his tales of wonder, his could-haves, and should-haves. With a weakness for the potato beer and prickly bitches, Drew grumbled on. It would be years before Hector understood any reasoning or fostered any respect for these survival methods that Drew conveyed to his fledgling son.

Now Maggie, Hectors Mam, was something else, a proper Queen. In fact, she was a proper Gin Queen. Whereas Drew could go without the potato beer for days and even weeks, Maggie danced the gooseberry gin trot all too well.

Maggie was a tiny specimen. She would sit like a butterfly on Hector's knee at teatime years later, jabbering of all she could have been and might be if Drew let her go.

Maggie had started life in the lowest burrows of the highlands, crowded and waterlogged, with eight to a nest and hunger at the door. Drew had been Maggie's escape, one rung up the ladder, not high enough to see the moon in the meadow beyond, but just enough to escape the drudge. With these odds against him stacked against the burrow wall as heritage, Hector was determined to go at least one more rung up that ladder.

The burden of legacy was not solely for the shoulders of Hector. Among the six others laid down on that hard floor in the burrow, there was only one that had lived through the next winter. His surviving sibling, a rare and beautiful wonder, Marge, was living proof that life may skip, trot and stumble beyond one's frail grasp. Small in stature and baring the rounded hedgehog hips, Marge had a mind like the edge of a pruning knife, capable of dueling at the speed of wasp's wings, destined to be the true champion of the family, if only she had taken the chances offered her.

Marge became a mother of sons, tall and strong, honorable and well done, forged and nurtured at her own expense. Never a word, for she lived in the very moment at all cost to herself.

Those others in Hector's tiny sibling brood, there were five that had escaped the challenges of mortal life by succumbing early to winters, rather than navigating through the flurries of snow that would ultimately turn to slush in the grey of winter. These ghosts would haunt the family and Mam as they traveled the furrows and hedgerows year after year.

Life at ground level was where it started, and Hector was the recipient of that all too common prize, that he now understood as mediocrity.

Hector headed out of the burrow and into the world. Skinny for his age, possessing the basics to survive, he depended more on his instincts than any real skills. Hector was a simple lad. He was strong in heart and fair enough of mind, a dreamer from whence a thought first entered his head. Music, lights, and action, but the call never came.

Resolved to trust fate and the opportunities cast aside by others, Hector decided to discover a life of adventure and love, a grand passion at all costs.

Hector started by laying down the foundation of being at home, wherever that may be, being at peace with that self that yearned to discover one's grand passion. He had an acceptance of self as complete, fulfilled, idealistic...

Something was missing.

Standing at the top of Sutter's Hill, Hector looked out toward the setting sun and wondered what lay out there, undiscovered, pulling him away from all he knew.

Only the purest of self is left to share, the tiniest

remnants of qualities that are of essence.

Risk to share it, or by vile revulsion, turn away

from that which you have discovered.

Chapter 2 – At Twenty

ector shuffled into the dark burrow that housed the slugs. Plump, glistening, mucus-covered blobs of flesh, more water than substance. Twisting, turning, luminous, ghost slugs that were the foundation of his daily livelihood. Hector understood that this was but a means to an end, a step in the direction of his dreams. Accepting the step was his personal challenge, not just the burden of the tasks at hand. With care, he sprinkled the feed of earthworm rings among this hungry brood, blessing them for their bounty, enticing them to grow fat and juicy.

"Plump up my lovelies," Hector whispered. "We go to market soon, and I will not encumber you with my ambitions, but you will feed those ambitions with your worth as you dance in the bellies of turtles, rats, and toads."

Watching his small farm herd squirm blindly around in aimless direction amid slime and dirt, Hector was accosted by an idea. He thought of the infinite possibilities he had in any given second compared to these sightless, slimy sheep. He wondered at the chances lost or gained between breaths, the opportunities missed or found in the blink of an eye and the sheer randomness of it all.

For almost two years Hector had run the farm, starting small, nurturing every translucent, bulbous slug himself. Hand-delivering the wriggling bundles to eager customers at half the cost that most would typically pay for such quality.

He had become that which he farmed. He withered sightless amid slime and dirt until it hurt. Now at twenty, the roar of the silence finally overwhelmed him.

There had to be more to life, out there beyond the river and the farm. His heart knew it.

Hector suffocated by the no-thing that sat in plain sight for most of his lifetime: loneliness. As full as he was of self, there was the void. Impulsively, with unfounded passion, Hector chose to travel, leaving his birthplace against all advice of elders and parents.

"There are dangers and unknowns awaiting you," they would say repeatedly. Hector shrugged off their concerns; the lure of adventure was too strong. This journey was inevitable.

The thrill of waking before dawn, a mysterious and quiet time that is covered in the darkest shroud of heavy velvet, soft, encompassing, with the slightest essence of light nipping at the edges. Hector packed his bag in the dark with the residual smell of the woodstove now heavy in the cold damp air of his burrow. Hector readied for the journey. Leaving the sanctuary of home, he stepped out into the moonlight just before dawn.

Hector scurried between century-old oak trees, dashing through the last of the moonlit shadows, avoiding the silent and fatal swoop of the owls. Through the thicket, over the stream that fed Sutter's Mill and down into the croft. As he traveled through the woods toward the wagon pick-up, Hector joined groups of other travelers making the same journey, each for a different reason.

Hiding under the fresh-packed straw once upon the wagon, the travelers settled in. Many creatures, faces, and eyes poked through the straw, most paws clutching little bundles, as the wagon rolled out into the coming dawn.

Hector's travel bag held soft slug jelly on pinecone kernels and small dark beetles, all to be washed down with chamomile tea, flavored with wild honey and a dash of mint he had picked fresh that morning as the dew had just begun to settle.

With warm tea in his belly and the rhythmic trundle of the wagon on the rough road, Hector drifted into a half-dream sleep.

He dreamt of walking among his favorite trees, deep in the forest, passing so many creatures, all colors, types, and creeds, all foraging, always foraging for the next meal, eyes to the ground, occasional glances skyward, trained on impending doom where the sharp talons of the gods hung omnipresent.

All manner of creatures rushed around foraging. The question whispered in a quiet voice through his dream, "What if we stopped and spoke when our eyes met? What if we shared with each other, our stories, hopes, dreams, and fears?" The voice whispered to him again, prompting him to wake.

It was nearing mid-morning, and the voice in the dream stayed with Hector long after he had scrambled down from the wagon just outside the village. It was all unfamiliar territory, new smells, different wind, and the promise of adventure.

Securing a hollow under the root of a large tree, Hector shared the last of his packed meal with a young mouse whose eyes darted back and forth amid quick bites of the slug-jelly-encrusted pinecone.

Hector gnawed at the small dark beetle he had pulled from his bag; it frothed when bitten into, crunchy, bittersweet. With tummies full, he and his companion set off to explore the nearby town of Millbury.

Hillary saw Hector shuffle into town that spring morning. His air was that of a traveler, a seeker. She had seen many come and go before. A small mouse, an unlikely companion, accompanied him.

From her flower stall, Hillary watched him skirt the edges of the market, coming to rest at the steps of the fountain. The set of his shoulders intrigued her; he seemed larger from afar, as she would later muse with her mother. Staring, she saw the deep searching etched across his face and wondered if one so young carried such a burden by choice.

He by all outward appearances seemed set in his ways, one among many that one perceives as complete and in control, the one that protests the need to be helped, or loved only slightly more than herself, she thought.

How ironic she thought that he was now her study in all that she knew existed, a young lost hedgehog walking into her town. From afar, he displayed that fragile line a leader keeps as they hold the reins many fear to take up. Reins to that indefinable steed of life, a beast of burden to some, a charger to others, wild and encapsulating all at once. Hopes and dreams undulating beneath its flanks and shining coat.

She imagined perfection in him with just the slightest flaw visible, making him real. The traveler needing to be vulnerable for acceptance opens his guard a little further than most might notice, inviting you in if you dare. This, entirely she saw in Hector at a glance, more instinct than solid fact. She stepped toward him.

As Hillary sauntered over to the fountain, she chanced a closer look. Dropping a small posy of yellow roses as she bustled by him, he bent to pick them up and offered them back to her.

He met her eyes and faltered. An unexpected thrill drove through Hector and rooted him to the ground.

What now lay exposed between them in a look caught his breath; a simple, gentle embrace could begin the journey. Hector leaned toward her, audaciously anticipating an embrace. Hillary danced lightly away into the crowd. His heart had stopped; he forced himself to breathe again.

Regaining his composure, his desires rallied around his fear. He gazed out over the heads of the crowded market. Hector's eyes darted back and forth, looking for the one he now knew he had come to find, the one he could not live without. An inevitable path he had stumbled upon so quickly, was this his true destiny unfolding before him?

All answers lie brooding beneath that thin veneer of dust that settles on life, a dust that makes great beauty slightly dull, the way a thought perceived through a veil of fear obscures a life better lived.

Reaching out by sheer will, Hector found her in the crowd. He touched her shoulder, trusting his intuition that what lay before them was a future.

Hillary turned and smiled knowing that joy, passion, and love were theirs should they choose to believe that exists unconditionally.

Hector's loneliness evaporated with that smile. A soft mist now dispersing, she led him to the most delicate place and bathed him, sweet and scented, casting off the years of doubt in an instant with her look. Was this an illumination of instincts when darkness dissolves, becoming light enough to make out the first faint shapes of love?

Thus, began the bristling of hairs and pounding of hearts. "I see you," he mouthed amid the noise of the marketplace, drawing his last breath of alone, now gone forever, and his first breath of together.

Hillary leaned forward and kissed him, drawing the breath from him.

The slightest leap, so small to the untrained eye, boundless and courageous to the fearful.

Love holds your breath when you step out into the abyss, now content to perish fulfilled, Hector thought if anyone had cared to ask.

"It is all quite different, compared to the best-laid plan," Hillary said as they talked over a picnic later that afternoon. "That brooding tangle of thoughts that placed you before me here," teased Hillary, reading the wonder on his face. "But lighter and oh, so clear now that the fearless leap has been taken after so long. So very long, and so much hand wringing."

Hector marveled at her words and drank deeply as she spoke, not sure if she read his mind or had seen his soul laid bare.

Four days later, they married. As they vowed to stay together under the moon and sun, Hector remembered something he had once heard, "It is not our abilities that define who we are, it is our choices."

Hector had made the first true choice of his life, the best choice of his life.

Now, at last, you know your gifts, small fruits

of life appear, others can see them too.

Choose now how to impart each, as all

have merit or consequence once

breathed out and shared...

Chapter 3 – At Thirty

Hector and Hillary set off one day just before dawn, a picnic, a day of discovery, an adventure, life beyond the apple grove. Worm sandwiches and grub pies packed into a woven basket lined with bluebird feathers.

They set off across the stream as sunlight popped her nose over the hills and wished them a good morning, with a promise to watch over them all day long.

Sitting on the hill in the shade of a single wind-worn tree, high above the meadow, Hector asked, "What has happened to me Hillary?" between bites of his worm sandwich, "What changed?"

"I once roamed these fields and woods with little thought for anything else other than turnip ale and a soft bed in which to wake. My head and heart were so full of deeds and lusts. I spent years gazing across rivers I feared to cross. Now look, here we sit in tall green grass, miles from home in a sunbaked glory, munching maggot pies, the world at our feet, and we are in love."

"This has happened to you," replied Hillary with a wry smile, as she rubbed her soft protruding belly. They will be here soon." Hector smiled and then cried, tears of joy at the sheer fact of being overwhelmed by the nature of things.

After clearing the picnic things away, Hector and Hillary began the journey home, holding hands and cradling the thought of their new family between them, laughing and talking of how wonderful the sunset looked as she bade them both goodnight until the new morning.

The pups came to them in the spring, a litter of two. Hector sat at the edge of the straw nest, watching Hillary twist and turn in the soft foraged bed of fresh herbs and grasses he had constructed for this day.

Hillary's mother had traveled and joined them, she stood now silently present, gently wiping Hillary's brow as the pains came and went.

A new emotion now engulfed Hector, one of complete uselessness, knowing that he could do nothing to sooth Hillary's pain. He had no ability to ensure the safe delivery into the world of his pending brood.

Hector realized, in fact, that he had little or no place in the discomfort emanating throughout the warm constricting burrow.

Like a ghost he hovered, desiring a simple manual task to quell the fear for Hillary's welfare, his primal urge to protect her and their babies.

His mother-in-law saw the familiar look and asked him to go fetch some water. Her wisdom evident to Hillary, now that she understood the value of distraction.

Upon returning, Hector heard the muffled squeaks and grunts. Approaching the nest in astonishment, he gazed at the pink and blind babies, like little blobs of paint on the soft bedding. They mewed and squirmed in random fashion, seeking the teat. A small litter, as was usual for the first of many that would be expected. An abundant legacy of procreation, the gift of bounty and one's natural right in the world.

Under the gentle touch of Hillary's mother, Oma with her singing words, Hillary laid exhausted and all used up. Drawing on all but the last of her energy, she shifted on to her side, presenting her teats to her babies. Blindly they found their instinctive destination and nestled in to feed. "A job well done, my love" Hillary's mother crooned as she soothed the dryness of Hillary's parched throat with a mixture of honey and the water that Hector had brought in.

Looking at Hector, she said, "Father, will you stoke the fire and brew some nettle tea? It is about time you were of some use."

"Father," Hector said below his breath. "Father. I am a Father!" Hector could not contain his joy of fatherhood. "I swear that I could be the first hedgehog in the world to behold this wonder. Look what we have made!" he shouted. "We are a family." Hillary turned and gave a faint smile, "Yes, a family."

"Tea, Hector," Oma commanded, forcing Hector from his stupor.

"Yes, tea. I will get it."

After the births, they settled into a burrow of Hillary's making, a new soft place, filled with the smells of what was now familiar as home, a place that quelled the desire to roam, and a place to live.

They flourished together, with the children to inspire them, growing tiny paws and gruff voices, sharpening spikes turning pink to brown. The seasons turned their cycle, and in autumn Hector reluctantly watched Hillary go. The flight of the bumblebees, he called it.

Hillary ventured forth into the old pastures of her youth, excited as she anticipated the welcome of sharing her pups, Sophie and Emma with her own family, brothers, sisters, and cousins; Hector had chosen not to go with them; the slugs needed tending.

Letting Hillary and the pups go beyond his reach was the hardest lesson Hector had endured in their time together thus far. That evening after they had left, Hector found himself wandering in the woods. He came upon a clearing, a small babbling brook fed by a spring running from the hillside near the burrow.

Stooping to drink, the water cleared, revealing an unexpected image, one that conveyed the depth and treasures of his life. Gazing into the pool, deeper and deeper, Hector saw Hillary and the children staring back, confirming his riches, sealing his commitment to the love they shared.

Reflecting on Hillary, Hector's mind wandered to the love and respect for her that he had grown into.

Like so many hedgehogs, she was genuinely protected on the outside by a spiky covering. However, soft, gentle, and vulnerable on the inside. "Just like most of us these days," he mumbled, "As we scurry through the weeds around us at ground level." Hector paused and thought back. When did he truly start to love her? How did he learn to love her?

Hillary would say if asked, that it started with that kiss in the square. Perhaps, Hector thought, that it was the day he had pushed her so far away, a month or so into their beginning, as he struggled to share his freedoms, making her the excuse for all his raw fears and doubts.

She, with no foothold or defense against his anger, his unreasonable buyer's remorse, fought back, baring teeth and clawing for survival, respect with grace when all seemed lost and curling up was not an option.

She had refused his fears and offered the alternative of contentment, of love and strength to stay the course.

So began the lessons that she would teach Hector every day, at times unaware of her ways, with a glance, a nudge, a subtle word, some not so subtle when needed. These gifts were evident in the family she had given him, the family she had made him a part of.

"Without her, there would be no us," Hector shared with the forest, a comfortable place to admit his failings, a solace where no one would hear. Understanding now that his fears were his strengths once they had been conquered.

After a long slow drink in the mysterious pool, Hector foraged around in the dirt for some tasty worms. The larder was now bare without Hillary there. Finding a few fat slugs and a crunchy centipede, Hector sauntered off, even swaggered a little in his contentment.

Up the hill to the burrow, he went, knowing that there were only two more sleeps until they came home. A big yellow and black bumblebee flew up, disturbed by this bustling stranger. Hector watched its awkward flight. Inspired, he sang a tune with words of his own making.

The Flight of the Bumblebee

"What is a house with no bums in it?

No bums to fill the chairs.

No wee bums to rustle around the burrow at

night. No bums in her nest full of her scent.

No bum lying next to me as the rain adds

a chill to the night air.

No bum to cuddle and pull to the curve of

my body made to fit as only her bum does.

No bums in our burrow makes it just a place

to be until you three bums return to me,

and the big yellow Bumblebee.

35

Always back to simple integrity.

The walls we build, high or low

defined by conscience.

Those transparent walls we can

hide behind or stand tall upon

Chapter 4 – At Forty

t forty, the roar of the silence overwhelmed Hector again. It had crept up, disguised in the years of pushing against the dull edges of his life, harder, harder, each day hoping to draw some blood, some sign of life. Hector felt himself suffocating again by the spectral no-thing, an immense mediocre shroud, draped in plain sight throughout his life, day after day.

Hector burrowed deep, well past the deepest he had ever dug before, scared, on new ground, in new ground. Darker, darker, the small light at the end of the tunnel looked like the moon high in the sky on a winter's night.

The earth cooled as he dug and the soil became harder, progress was slow. Hector felt the press of the earth around him bear down, looming, still, blindly he dug. That moon had now disappeared from the sky behind him and finally, exhausted, he reluctantly allowed instinct to drive direction. That is when things began to change.

Solitude engulfed him, now entombed by his own design. Hector paused, drew breath, and looked straight ahead. A hard surface poked from the earth - solid rock. Up, down, left, right all in a single thought. Frantic with progress halted, Hector placed his wet snout on the cold hard stone. Had he been here before, too many times?

He had set off from the burrow just hours before, an attempt at finding a new direction, a new reason for his dreams, a new objective, and a transition. Why now did it all seem so familiar? Safety, instinct, fear all creating a mask that he had put on so willingly, so quickly, by denial. By default, he had sold himself to the lowest bidder: doubt.

Hector contemplated an alternative: back to the security of the known from which he had run, a safe landing with no risk, a failure in others eyes, this obstruction hidden in plain view, yet concealed deep below one's goals and aspirations.

"Whom do we win for, should success be the better goal?" Hector said into the hard surface that blocked his progress, "Winning means someone must lose."

Hector realized that the rock would always be there, back or forward, because the world demands bigger, better, faster, more. Snout pushed up against the rock, Hector felt his breath in the cool air. He was dressed in spikes, hundreds of visible barbs, designed to repel an attack. Scurry, bustle, sharp teeth and wit at the ready the ultimate defense, "useless against yourself" he murmured and then laughed aloud in the thick darkness.

Second to running away was to coil up in a tight ball, hoping the invisible attacker that he knew as doubt would leave.

All these defenses were instinctual, a product of his nature. A legacy of his heritage, and the tools of his physique. Who he was or should be. Hector closed his eyes and lay down on the floor of the burrow, exhausted. Eventually, his breathing slowed. Deep heaves of his chest consumed him. Eyes fluttered to shut, allowing sleep to take him on a fitful dream journey.

In Hector's dream, all never went quite as planned. Years of belief that things would get better! Years running on the treadmill of expectation and consumption, sheer brute force of will driving him on toward perfect. Anything to attain the desired outcome of bigger, better, more. Hector listened to the archive of grand declarations reverberating in his head: "I will, I must, you shall, we want, we need."

In the swirling fog of the dream, Hector saw himself green-eyed with frustration as he stomped through the daisy field, oblivious to the damage he caused.

A slight nagging consciousness buried deep in the recess of his being, boxed and sealed, safe revealed itself and chewed on the mindless carnage he caused in the name of desire.

In this dream, he had it all, wealth and fame. Yet the two simple things he truly wished for most had eluded him: Love and Joy. Love on so many levels: the love of a wife, a child, a friend, a parent, a sister or a brother, given day after day when they believe in you. Or a quiet love that holds you up under the weight of bitter days. Joy found in obvious places: the joy your child gives you by holding onto a hug longer than expected, for no reason. A joy of a friend's smile, when seeing you across a field, they change direction to visit with you. The proud love shown by a parent in a simple gesture as they watch their grown baby rant and rave at the world. Reaching out, gently touching them, wordless, reassuring, and unconditional after so many years of necessary conditions.

The joy of self, the deepest and most unforgiving love, the love we fear yet desire the most. For there is no ambiguity, no mask to show to the very self, naked, the reflection is honest. You can run but not hide, from self.

Hector saw himself as he sat in his expansive burrow, filling only the space he occupied in the old overstuffed chair. He pulled again on the pipe stuffed with chamomile tobacco and let his breath ebb out slowly, watching the smoke twist and turn as life had, up and out. Away it drifted from him.

Hillary had drifted away in much the same manner. One day he had breathed her out, and she had moved on, grateful to be free of his frustrations, his rage, and his discontent. On the wind, she drifted to those greener pastures filled with daises she knew how to nurture.

Sophie and Emma would at times, stop by with their respective broods accompanied by an overwhelming noise that could not be quelled, regardless of how much elderberry wine Hector consumed.

Most knew that it was time to leave when Grump-paw started to take misaimed kicks at the squabbling pups, his own grandchildren. They simply stopped visiting. Hector understood that in this dream, he had indeed survived like this and would now die like that. Free of the burden of love, alone and joyless.

The realization struck. Amid huffs and haw's Hector's discontent would finally consume him. He saw himself leaving a note under a bottle of gooseberry wine, written in his clumsy hand. He had placed the note around Hillary's little book, the one with the faded covering of embossed flowers and scribbling, which had been constructed with care so long ago. The note read...

My Life at Ground Level...

Joy just flew out the window. After so long trying to hang on to it, I found I could no longer muster the strength required. It slipped from my grasp like fine sand; I cared less to see it go.

It was a relief, to say the least. Hanging on to that elusive emotion, smiling insincerely just to save face, as it was too hard.

Along with joy went happiness and peace as I raged at them for failing me. Good riddance.

Let me wallow in my stew. Contentment hung around, pretending to be a companion in my newfound freedom, but it too soon tired of having no one to play with, as I sat facing the wall mumbling to myself.

I searched high and low for remorse, but there was none to be found. It had all been consumed in the journey here, to this bleak, dark place. So now, all I can see is loneliness sitting in the vast dark hole in my chest. It weighs me down so much that I cannot lift from this seat, nor raise my eyes above the wall before me.

I thought that it would be different, more joy, much more joy. There was once passion, but I let that go so very long ago without realizing that it was the beginning of my demise. I traded it for gold and a promise of greener grass that never came true.

I know now where they all are Joy, Passion, Happiness, and Peace, - but the road from here looks too long and with a sigh, I slump back into this chair, bidding you farewell... Hector.

Waking with a start, Hector was chilled and stiff in the damp burrow, he took a moment to realize where he was.

The dream gripped his chest.

Was this an inevitable result of his discontent?

Was there any choice?

Was this his future?

Another choice? Another desire?

No need to change his size or shape, no reason to dull his spikes.

No desire to face the true nature of an attack when it came. A choice to perceive, rather than coil up, always missing the chance to embrace rather than thwart, or discard. It was time to give up the nocturnal darkness, time to indulge in the light of the sun without the threat of swooping hawks or wayward dogs. Time to stand in the meadow, breathe the green grass, and pull dragonflies from the air.

Here now, sitting at the end of the dank, lonely tunnel, Hector saw a glimmer of light in his own mind's eye, a path home.

He had allowed himself to be consumed by his own desires and misfortunes, fooled by his own frustration at opportunities not taken. His own realization now was simple. Hector had forgotten what truly mattered in life: love and awareness of the boundless gifts that immersed him in that life. He realized that he was not sinking, but awash with infinite possibilities.

The dream had shaken him deeply; he saw it as a reprieve. An alternative he could create if he stopped digging to nowhere. Imagining his family asleep in the home burrow, he sighed, how sweet to nestle among them, content.

Stiffly Hector got to his feet and stretched his weary bones, relieved at how untangled his thoughts seemed to have become. Bumping his head against the rock, Hector felt it give a little, shift. The large, flat stone tumbled to the floor, a thin veneer of stone, not the boulder he had assumed. With fresh earth exposed, any direction lay open to him now, should he take it.

"Another day perhaps," he voiced as he turned in the darkness to make his way back up the tunnel. It was night outside as Hector emerged. Had he been gone so long, chasing what-ifs yet again?

Passion comes in many forms, Hector reflected, as he breathed deep the smell of possibilities that hung in the night air. He barked loudly into the darkness "dreams should never die under the weight of others' assumptions and our own misdirected feelings of inadequacy." Then he set off home at a brisk pace, almost a jaunty trot if seen from afar.

Arriving at the burrow, he scooped up a paw full of crispy cricket wings from the bowl Hillary kept as a welcome near the entrance, Hector wondered what the future could hold if pursued fearlessly.

The glowworm began to fade, and Hillary stirred upon the straw-lined nest.

"Did you find it?" she asked. "Find what?" Hector whispered. "The ghost you were chasing." "Yes," Hector said. "It finally found me and told me a story of choice." He let out a long slow breath.

"I realized that I could have disappeared today, simply gone in an instant. Some may have wondered, I hope. Many would have just gone on with their day with the slightest ripple of me brushing against their memories. Then fading like a wisp of smoke upon the breeze, I would be gone forever."

"I understand," Hillary whispered back.

Hector felt the warmth of her breath on his snout, and with that, he fell into a deep, quiet sleep.

Slowly a light emerges, opening my nature to
all that I have become, all that I always was.
Little paths of light guide me should I choose
to follow this stumbled upon destiny amid
bluebirds and swallows.

Chapter 5 – At Last

ector sat on the grass outside the burrow, face to the sun. For many days now, with the dream on his mind, he had trudged back and forth without really noticing the small white and yellow daisies flowering around him, surrounding his everyday life: humble, insignificant yet abundant, and beautiful. From afar, or from above, they all looked the same. Naturally yellow and white, spread out in an even blanket around him in the meadow.

The day was warm, and Hector slid down to his belly and placed his snout on the ground, stopping for a moment.

He looked a little closer at the blanket of flowers in which he lay. Hector was surprised, all around him were the little flowers, some tall, some short, some thick, some thin, some a little whiter, some a little greener around the different hues of yellow in the center. Little faces of sunshine looking at him, all smiling freely.

One tiny flower made him think of wee Emma when she was a child, just green and budding with life, enchanted with all things around her in the forest.

Another flower caught his eye, a straggler, pushing above the others, vibrant and bright, calling, "Look at me."

His Sophie, splendid and independent and free-willed.

Yet another flower stood out, this one a slender beauty, standing slightly alone from the indistinguishable clumps. Hillary, he thought, in full bloom and blowing in the breeze back and forth in time with the earth. Other faces now appeared amid this blanket of nature, this blanket of friends, family, loves, and long-lost memories.

Reflections of all past and present, the abounding gifts he never noticed, so nearby, revealed through a veil just beyond his eyes, hidden behind his hurry, fragrant reminders of his dreams and loves.

Gently Hector picked the faces of pure sunshine and gave each a name, from the earliest memories to the end of today, when he had watched his grandchildren play around the entrance to the burrow. With this bed of flowers, he wove a chain, one by one, memory by memory. Hector was surprised by the length of this chain of life, a string of shining faces, each touching his heart, interlocked across his lifetime.

Occasionally Hector wove in another straggler, slightly brown from the sun, a little imperfection in the sea of perfection.

"That's how life is," Hector said, speaking to his creation. "More good than bad, I say." Wandering back through the meadow, daisy chain in hand, smoking slowly on elderberry leaves in his old clay pipe, paws feeling the earth caress him as the sunset against the hills.

Hector thought it funny how a few flowers could open the eyes and open the soul. Hector hung the simple band of woven dreams over the entrance to the burrow, a safeguard for the loved ones inside, thankful for these memories that had brought him here, blossoms in his heart. Holding his breath, Hector stepped a deliberate step forward. "It is all quite different compared to the plan, that brooding tangle of thoughts that has brought me here." He laughed, "Nevertheless, lighter and oh, so clear now that the fearless leap had been taken, after so long, so very long with much hand wringing."

Hector soared now, "I shall live unbound, for I have discovered that the grass is indeed greenest where you are."

You are light to me, the brightest light of all,

that light when I am still, fills every edge of

my being, I have blocked the brilliance with

my own shadow at times, now years cannot

diminish its brilliance and our love.

Chapter 6 – At Fifty

At fifty contentment sat lightly on Hector's shoulders, an ease he had fought against for far too long.

Having one's slug and eating it was a desire he no longer pursued. There was a pure joy in the life that he now lived. Days where he felt an acceptance of his lot in life. A comfort in his own skin, a respect for the past and an eager, boyish anticipation for the future. That future, he once feared, was now a more straightforward way forward in the present. Hillary had been home from the market a day or two after Hector's discovery of her little book and the snout-rubbing meeting in the burrow entrance.

A gentle shift had happened. The fragrance of it hung lightly in the air. Hillary's presence seemed to have filled every nook and cranny of the burrow, like the smell of baking or how the sound of laughter swelling one's chest in hearty revelry, a deep intake of breath that makes you relish the thought of living a thousand years in love.

Here now, in his large overstuffed chair, Hector sat breathing all of it in, drawing from the air in each breath an understanding of the fine line between passion and reason, that grey area he had fallen in and out of his whole life. Never finding the balance to see that it was a place of vibrant color.

A place where all lives in balance.

Hector thought of the slug farm. sold to the highest bidder, there had been no shortage of offers for his life's work. All that effort now seemed worth it. The reasoning, the steadfast loyalty, responsibility to all but self, the frustration, and the questions gnawing at his gut year after year, that he had endured, had overcome, had embraced.

"They" had said, and he had done.

Years pitted against his passion, and now he had let it go, now free to explore the color that was always so close at hand yet hidden by his own perspective.

The children, well grown with broods of their own, came and went as they pleased, fruitful, season after season. Hillary relished the hustle and bustle, the caring and warmth that surrounded her.

An abundance of life bloomed in the hedgerow. Little squeaks and grunts with slugs, spiders, and worms to eat and play with. Hector watched the chaos and imagined another little tale to tell, a story to share at bedtime with this noisy rabble. Picking up a notebook, he opened it urgently to capture his thoughts before they flew away on graying wings.

His passion had always been in writing, anything to let the mind wander. Boundless stories of imagining, life lived in a million different ways, so far from the limiting wanderings of fear.

Possibilities all wrapped up in the joy of sharing in delicious vulnerability one's deepest thoughts, real or imagined. Summer brought warmth and long walks. Rising from his chair as Hillary entered the burrow, Hector asked her if she cared to wander a while with him upon their hills. Slower now, Hector and Hillary leaned on each other as the hills grew steeper before them. The sun sent out her greeting with a warming smile.

Sitting down below their tree, rabbit hair blanket, mulberry wine and munching maggot pies, the view of their world wrapped around them in the gentlest embrace.

"What has happened to me?" Hector asked Hillary.

"I have happened to you, so long ago, when you found me by a fountain in a village far away. I am still here. And you now older after so much hand wringing shall write me another story."

Hector laughed as Hillary wiped crumbs from his chin and kissed him on the snout. She placed her head on his shoulder. "Only if we write the next story together," Hector said. "You know how the story ends."

Hillary laughed as she took Hector's paw and lifted her face up toward the sunshine. With eyes closed, she said, "This story has been more than enough for me, but let me think, this time we will start with a happy ending where the grass is greenest. I will start with my Ode to Joy – At sixty."

I see you some days in full flight, prancing and springing through my life, reflecting in the eyes of my loves, soaring high with my heart at your side, attached to your every move and action, pulling me along to that very place I seek... Joy!

I cannot find you on those dark days I fear. You dance at the edge of my vision, just out of sight, just out of reach, more a lost feeling than a reality. Frustrated, I cannot deny you exist, out there, so near, yet elusive... Joy!

I will wait here or seek you out this very now, the moments of every day, in eyes and embraces, in hearts, both theirs and mine, for you are only elusive when I forget to live fully in you... Joy!

Hillary smiled, packed up the picnic, and said, "Let's go home."

Hector laughed again and said, "Yes, let's. I would enjoy that."

The End for now

Ramblings –

Ramblings –

Hillary tiptoed around the burrow. It had been a full and adventurous day. The family had visited for the summer solstice, and she had watched Hector teach the pups how to dunk for apples in the pond.

Hector lay asleep now, snoring as deeply as he had drunk the honey wine. She removed his glasses and picked his writing book out from beneath his paws that lay crossed on his belly as it rose and fell with each breath. His face, smooth in sleep, looked youthful, at peace. She sighed. His journal, tatty and worn, fell open in her paws. She paged through, reading snippets of his journey. She felt content in knowing that he loved that she read his ramblings. There was no better or honest critic than love.

A Wee Kiss

A wee kiss o' you wherever you be, is all that

makes a man o' me, for life's true rights bonds he

and she, as man is man and delightful thee.

But still confused wherever you be, as all

abounds for, I am me. Too soft, too real for ye to

see, and really just wanting to be free,

and in love with thee.

Snow

Make haste and come to me,
for I fear that I will lose your vision
in my mind's eye.
I close my eyes to the falling snow
outside and let its pure crystal flakes
rest against the hills and fields of
my roaming soul.
Fall hard and thick. Bury me deep
in your love, from where I shall rise,
cast off winter's slumber,
radiating this warmth I know as love.

Strife

On this road of life, I encounter naught but

strife, and think to take a wife.

Choose the road and wander if I must,

for in life's travels I vent my lust.

For freedom's sake I make mistakes,

reputation built, possessions I take.

Believe in I, rich for who, me or you,

heart fulfilled by whiskey's brew.

Happy now, I live a steady pace, feign a smile

that hides my fall from grace.

Night-Night

I kiss everyone in my burrow goodnight.

Behind the shroud of darkness, I watch life still

to slumber. Wishing all well I wander off to sleep

restlessly until tomorrow starts anew – thinking.

The hardest part of receiving love is being able to

return it with an equal sense of wanting.

The saddest part of receiving love is not having

the same love to return.

Who gives, who takes?

Cry and Huff

I as fool devoid of grace, rush right

in for all love's sake.

Seeking it, that elusive trust which starts

Joy and lovely lust.

Makes of me cry and huff when in I rush,

push and shove against nature's thrust.

Drawing on desire and simple trust,

while forgetting the feeling, living stuff.

In the dance I beg a simple crust,

defining what is to do and what is must.

Would Be

Can't spell, got no grammar,

failed school and have a stammer.

Have a brain and good opinion,

street smart and done some livin.

Question why and write it down,

research the facts that I've found.

Life is short and feelings long;

I'll have no legacy when I'm gone.

Dig down deep, reach that place from

where once came such honest faith.

Live to fight another day.

Tuckered

Wee pink knickers and rosy cheeks.

Plumb well tuckered out, and in deep sleep.

Scoop her up and off to bed, on my shoulder

bumps a weary head.

Lay her down and tuck her tight,

no bed bugs will bite tonight.

Whisper love in dream filled ears,

hope to God that she will hear.

In years to come she'll forget our hours

I watch her sleep, my little flower.

Two Haggis

It's a strange pair we are!
Bonded by birth as father and son.
Forged as adversaries through a twisted fate,
yet hopeful as equals when we learn to back
down from our fears and wishes.
Our Celtic blood fires the forge of heated
encounters. Twisting and pulling the metal
of our soul, close but never touching long
enough to bond.
But entwined we are by fate and blood alike,
each expecting more of the other,
and getting less.

Sausage

Little stinker!

Sausage bum.

How are you my little one?

Little monster!

Magic sun.

You are how my life begun.

Little terror!

Tender fun.

You are my hearts sum.

Little sausage, little sun, you are the one

for me and mum.

Real

Made not of iron, stone nor steel,

but of spikes and flesh, made real.

Why hide those feelings we fear revealed?

Made of doubt, hate or fear,

we draw on all that causes tears.

So why seek or chase love away when "I love you"

falls in empty space?

Made within a beginning place,

as love's journey builds, pace by pace.

So learn to show our colors bright,

now love dawns, we see daylight.

Little Bird

I know now of walk away, for when love dies,

no reason to stay.

But we as fools devoid of grace would

for love's sake lose all face.

So, broken hearted seek love anew,

reconstruct as fools will do.

Fatal love begun again, as our last cry

is when love when.

Little bird of yellow and blue, may each be as

true as you, for nature's trust is life for you,

but mortal hearts trust less or few.

Brave Face

I want to cry out loud, full heart-felt weep.

Let out all the years of held in tears,

pent up for social standing, flow.

Curl up as a pup and have tummy stroked,

as mother should have done through

skint-knee years.

First love's brokenhearted sobs held in

so tight to save needing another's touch.

The tears held in when death stops at your door,

brave false face shuns the loss.

Life is due to begin when first tears fall.

Deep

Anger swells deep inside, all because of stupid

pride. For what is right as we think,

but in truth does not all stink?

It will take time to heal the pain, this dull and

deep refrain, for release we choose internal weep

until next time we solemn meet.

Pour out on this page, soak up this infernal rage,

release my love from the cage. The road ahead

seems long and empty as I seek more;

fear gains me less than plenty.

Mine

Soft and tender entwined.

So close together makes you mine.

Life and love or death and hate as we conspire

to cast our fate. Each step well placed on heart

or soil, it is we who will weep or toil.

If I were of life to ask a gift, it would be

that love flow between us eternally this.

We both reach out, no holding back in love's

new spark that once kept fragile hearts apart.

Dizzy

Hearts change in full moon's light,

eyes glow back, love's dizzy height.

Close to earth on grassy seat, we reach,

embrace, lips now meet.

Stories told and secrets shared, open hearts

nurture a promise of care.

Honest truth is all it takes to forward move,

leaving hurt and hate.

A gentle kiss determines fate

and so to you my pledge I make.

Sister

A sister is a wonderful thing, watch her laugh,

hear her sing, when all around would lesser

mortals to their knees bring.

A sister is a treasured thing, holds you up when

all would cave and crash about, with doubtful

thoughts or there about.

A sister is the other half, from the same of birth

right cast. No judge of things possessed is she,

for when you are lost, she offers a place to just be.

Great

I thought I would be great, a shining star.

Truth be told, I may not have tried that hard.

Hanging hats on idle thoughts.

Lofty dreams on soaring spire tops.

Greatness is a state of mind.

Dreams made best at one's own shrine.

Looking around I see life's great work.

Full of choice, enough is never enough.

Like the moon, I glow at times bright.

Reflecting the lives of all who might.

Pay

Pay the toll and pass the gate, all of this is only

fate. Cast your boat to shore anew,

let no doubt follow you.

Pay with joy this meager sum, it may seem large

to all or one, but in the cast of life's full net,

we see it but a little bet.

Pay regard for all you've had, sleeping soft

to the songs of nature's bard.

Life will on and is called hard,

but you may travel wide and far,

playing the best of your dealt card.

Rock

Our Passion is not the same, the rock you are

for purposes, standing solid in the running

river of my distractions.

The river's ebb and flow, causing me to

crash against you.

You, that solid rock you are, holding us firm

with no desire to drift in the racing current.

Hold me fast here with you, lest my passions

drift and I am lost, adrift, alone.

Door

Cross that threshold, put aside your fears,

take reluctant steps tainted by desire

and intrigue.

Memories of pleasure still lingering

with the scent of a recent past,

not yet stale at the dawn of another day.

One parting kiss, a simple request,

gently instructed, demanded, reluctant,

obediently bowing to that embrace.

Once crossed, all is new and possible.

Now

So, now is here. It never was, it raced ahead in
life's wild rush. Never quite the dream I sought,
always just one more thought away.
So, now is here again, can I brave the test,
the test of time, for now is none, no future,
no past, no present.
It is the very now a slice of heaven.
Embracing the moment, I am here,
still and ready for the next moment,
and the next, one at a time.

Can't Hide

No place left to hide, looking, listening

to your own preaching at last.

Fear, now shoving the options out

in front of you as a soft landing.

Eyes darting as they gaze into you again and

again, and you let them, openly engaged.

Stand shoulder-to-shoulder, entering this

new phase, the new waits as boundless.

Who knows what you will become?

Make that fearless leap.

The Beast

Hold your tongue, that slippery beast,

betrayer of thoughts, boaster of egos,

a whip of wit that kills souls in a word.

Wild horses of voice, cascade forth

in a verbal deluge, spewing.

Thoughts of my own making,

running free within and without.

Looking down on oneself always leaves

destruction in its wake, viewed as perception

by the self for my soul's sake.

Be gentle.

Words

Barbaric words from whence I came,

honest words scream again.

Carrot dangling on the line,

drunken words reflecting time.

Make me beg, enjoy my pain,

same old story, same refrain.

Golden coins to ease the pain,

the price of ransom paid again.

Hostage to hope and fear,

your subtle jabs will bring no tears.

A price too high for you to pay,

grow old now and fade away.

Gone

So silent the hour before dawn, even my own

thoughts need quieting as they pulse with the

rhythmic beat of my heart, the only sound above

the scratching of my pen on paper.

Creaks and groans of the moving earth

around me, roots growing when

no one should be watching.

Children stretch and whimper in their sleep.

Silent, my mind wanders and fills with

possibilities, thoughts ebbing out onto

the page for my children to read when

I am dead and no more.

Everything

How do you know when you have everything

you might ever need to make the journey of life?

Realizing that I did not want to live alone

anymore was first.

Who would I wake with and laugh with

as we embrace, was next?

To feel someone, move around and be so close,

even a room away was last.

This is everything needed for the journey.

Running

Do I pack and run away,

pray self for now to stay?

Work and play, no decision given,

each his own, choose living.

Reasons here, reasons there,

end results, conclusions bare.

Try and fall, stand again, and in time

all leads to heartache's pain.

Decisions made cause life ahead.

Be calm, be reasonable, and use your head.

Daddy

Daddy rules, Daddy's way

Must I live for thee, night through day

Mummy lost, Mummy's song, must

you live through years long gone?

Sister, Daughter, Brother, Son,

two loving hearts taunted as one.

Mummy loved, now distant one,

hold no key to hurts yet undone.

Desire, fate, belittled self,

cannot sit on that lifeless shelf.

Straighten up, push past aside,

move on forward where living breeds life.

Right

The jolly day of which I write is by

no means real or moral right.

So why must I, as gods may say,

be pure and true to all each day?

Foolish heart, I write of joy,

that of which I do avoid.

I know it lives in easy reach,

first steps are mine to simply seek.

Trembling hands grasp and beg for

contented life beneath the hedge.

Fiddly Dee

Tally ho and while away,

see me waste yet another day.

Tally hi and tally ho, what fate of life

and where to go?

Tally hee and fiddly dee,

what shall become of unhappy me?

Basic words for basic fears,

how well I hide complicated tears.

Sleep will come now as I slumber,

all I want is to avoid this plunder.

Where are you now, my heart wonders?

Sunday

To be seen as strong, unchallenged and free,

reflects a truth, seen, as I lie entwined and safe

within your embrace, Sunday and soft.

What kiss is as real and touch so strong when

both decide to give the touching of eyes at dawn,

Sunday and dark?

Imagine strong, unchallenged and free,

yet weak in your embrace,

resting on Sunday and light.

Stories

I have stories written on scraps of paper hidden

in book covers and written in margins

of those same books.

The stories are fiction and fact, realities

and imaginings. The lines blur as stories are

woven by instinct, little nuances

extrapolating out into many pages.

A moment as observer molds into participant. A

voyeur of experiences imagined,

seldom lived and reluctantly felt.

I write my escape to be yours.

Hillary closed and kissed the little book. She tucked it into the side of the big leather chair where Hector would find it when he awoke.

She felt lighter and oh so clear now that the fearless leap had been taken, after so long, so very long with much hand wringing.

Epilogue –
At Sixty and Beyond

It was years later when Hector turned Sixty that Hillary collected up all of the notebooks and scraps of paper around the burrow. The old and new ramblings having expanded out into a simple form of poetry that Hector would not give a name to. He had settled into himself a little more. They would share his words together on still summer nights at the burrow entrance where years before they had discovered one another. Acorn toast drizzled with thick green caterpillar juice, squeezed out fresh and sprinkled with crispy gnats' wings.

"I had a little book made for your birthday," Hillary whispered in Hectors ear as they nuzzled. "Pick out one for me and read it, please."

Hector ran his paw over the raised lettering on the soft leather cover of the book Hillary handed to him. She always seemed to know. He looked at the clock on the wall, it sat at 6:22pm.

Where the grass is greenest
by Hector McNiesh.

Inside there was an inscription.

All answers lie brooding beneath that thin veneer of dust that has settled on our life, a dust that makes great beauty real, much the same way a thought perceived through a gossamer screen of hope reveals a life better lived, embellishing one's perspective, fueling reality and contentment at having more than enough.

I love you. You silly old wart – Hillary XXX

Foraging

It is the letting go of things that is hardest,

The epiphany as we learn

Nurture the gentler aspects of our

existence and ourselves

Perspectives that have been neglected

for far too long

It's not the finding of things anew to cling to,

But the discovery of desires that can be relished

As elemental to one's existence

I see them now, and perhaps reveal myself

In reciprocation for a fragile trust

A truce of sorts for all the years of battle

I raged in defense of long held beliefs.

Notions that now seem redundant

perpetuating the vicious circles, I fed them with

Searching, always searching,

all the way back to moments

That never worked in the first place.

Perhaps in letting go

I could consider that being was the beginning

Of exploring a life rather than chasing it

Discovered amid fields dusted with snow

Muddy banks where chocolate colored

Geese are Perfect foraging pairs.

Dancer

Conformity or deformity

Twisting out of shape

Appease others

Suppressed am I

Subtle nuances

Reduced am I

Conspire or Inspire

Slipping into nature

My own humanity

Mortal man am I

Excesses of life

Consumed am I

Reflection or deflection

Destiny defined anew

Legacy grasped

Dancer am I

Another life

Free am I.

Invisible Light

Sometimes,

If you're lucky to be at the right place

at the right time,

If you're attentive and open, you might notice

a small beam of sunlight slipping through

a little crack, in the world.

A universe of tiny particles normally invisible

to the eye, dance like magical silver glimmering

before your outstretched hands.

So lively and busy that you can almost hear

them shiver among each other and feel

their gentle touch on your skin.

You pause and acknowledge that a little gift

has just been given to you,

and that there is actually more.

More than you are able to comprehend.

It was how he had always imagined her.

And there she was in the dawn of his life.

Stand or Run

Stand and face the open sea.

When it washes cool over feet

Enjoy the ease of it. Or step away

Stand and face the open sea.

When this love began anew

We believed in it. Or found a way

Stand and face the open sea.

When in rising wraps your waist

Stand strong against it. Or lean away

Stand and face the open sea.

When it turned to grey

We were lost in it. Or taken away

Stand and face the open sea.

When it crashes over your head

Your breath is lost to it. Or swim away

Stand and face the open sea.

When crying eyes immerse

We are dead in it. Or drifting away

Remember the open sea that started this Love.

Dessert

I am over fear

Caution nips at my heels

Spinning to kick - I lose balance

On doubtful days

Sunshine on my face

I am square to the wind

Open to all - Pen to paper

Reflecting surroundings

Safety net irresistible

I know where they are

Obvious habits discarded

One last time

Easy solutions dusted off

Self as a war cry - Compromise in fear

Headlong Into mediocrity

From whence I came

Reformatting to fit - Fingers spread out

Pen in hand as promised

A blend of compromise

Just for today - Seeking inspiration

Something lighter of beauty

Humor creeps out

Spilling on the page

Over the edges

Like cream pie.

Nuance

Do you believe anything I say?

Can you see the subtle nuances of deception?

My eyes or the taunting lilt to my voice

I draw you in

It is not my intent it is my nature

I am seduced as much by these fabrications

Sincerity amid declarations of doubt

Concern for a compromise into mediocrity

For you are light to me, the brightest of all

Light that when I am still fills me whole

I want to bask in the full beauty of you

As you draw me in

There are times I smother the light

with my darkness

I block out the brilliance in fear

and misunderstanding

Photos of years blazing past cannot diminish

Concern that I failed to see the wonder

Moments now gone forever, believe me

When it was good here

It was best.

Move On

Shadows may linger in our minds

Thoughts moves on

Dreams flash and die if not acted upon

Belief moves on

Few old friends live at the same address

Life moves on

Buildings fall and the landscape changes

Creation moves on

Overgrown hills give testament to the past

Nature moves on

Paths once traveled hide under dust of days

Time moves on

Chart new courses and adventures

he moves on.

Incognito

My back against the tree, bright in the sunshine

The quiet moment stretched into an hour

A delicious hour that was mine alone

My upturned face relished the sun

as I slid into slumber

Lighter in my reprisal

Ready to cast off old damp coats that had hung

about me for too long

I started the walk back

to my sanctuary reflecting

Now it was time, I suppose.

She had been right in some way.

I hated to admit it, especially to her.

She represented in every way my nemesis

My scaffold of self-imposed deception

Weaving precariously under the weight

of my heritage

I could now redefine my legacy

Traveling incognito for so long

Was no longer the burden it needed to be.

Sweet Light – Delicious 1

It is simply the silence,

A delicious silence that envelops me

Thick it tastes upon my being

Punctuated only when I turn a read page

Disturbing the listless pet that warms

my feet at the end of the couch

Not a whisper do I hear

The sun swaps its own orange hue

on silhouette hills for moonlight

Rising moon across the valley in silence

her fullness illuminates

The sky resonates deep shadows amid yelps of

Fox pups

Greet the lustrous moonlight to hunt by

Crackling of wood smoldering

To flame as cast iron hearth creaks expanding

Warmth creeps silently around

filling the still room

Cold air chased out into the night

in reverence to my sanctuary

My respite that is now home

on gentle rolling hills

Perhaps I shall be reckless

Allow the kettle to boil and whistle

alongside croaking frogs

A cacophony that is nature and really

no noise at all

Symphony of molasses undulating around me

Sleep comes easy as I set my book down.

Well

There is nothing in the well but

vapors of responsibility

Commitment hangs heavy in the air

Pressing down on hunched shoulders

There is nothing in the well

that compares weighted hearts

Pulling self up from the depths of despair

Avoid the harsh explanation in daylight

There is nothing in the well you would recognize

No substance to the look in eyes

There is nothing in the well - Nothing.

Big Sky

Across the air - Whispered voices

Gentle words spoken - Unexpected moment

Warm bed sleeping - Butterflies awakened

Shed your skin - Covered with breath

Molded in curves - Fragrant hair

Desire roused now - Sleep content

Reluctant is departure - Promise return...

Snow 2 – The Chase

Make haste and come to me

I fear to lose you in my mind's eye

Pray may I ask in humble ignorance

I close my eyes to the snow

Pure flakes fall against me

Against hills and fields

To what extent will you intrigue

Obtainable or challenge

Long stride over stones

I am buried deep consumed

No hope to rise in spring

Husky voice and spiky clad

Radiating warmth ephemeral

Resurrect under cover of dark

One fateful kiss to span

Decades pass in slow motion

Autumns discovery anew

Now in winter we seek spring.

Trusted

Hearts and moods change in moonlight

Eyes glow back spirits dance

Trusted visit tests romance

Close to earth on wooden seats

Quiet streets, whiskey chasers

Trusted clock is a racer

Stories told and secrets shared

Open hearts from shame or fear

Trusted friend holds all as dear

Temptation rises alongside breath

Holding back doth dance protest

Trusted past now distressed

Passions moment may declare

Weeks or months of love employ

Trusted now in pure joy

A gentle kiss determine makes

On bridge or bed, you do impale

Trusted hours behind the veil

High moons light through silken hair

Small soft tummy caressed with care

Trusted I lay my hand there

Honest truth is all it takes

To forward move leave hurt to fate

Trusted words we must relate.

Mundane

Love me she blurts

Words that struggle for purchase

Unsteady ground

Her declaration of unrequited

Affections mundane

Futile in encumbered state

Emotional frailty

Apart

I love you he reacts

Unsteady him amid grasping

Soft underfoot

His epiphany of her profound

Intimacy mundane

Euphoric now statement made

Liberated strength

Together.

Resurrection

Wake up, wake up.

Arise from that stupor you bask in

Liberate desire from conformity.

Cast off the heavy blanket of domestication

Stand up and walk out into the spring.

Wake up, wake up.

Cast no shadow of past days

Sun overhead at noon allows the gift of time

Feel the lightness of feet and leap forth

Resurrection is upon you and inevitable

Wake up, wake up.

Options are thick about you if received

Honesty is the only cost needing expression

Denial of possibilities in fear is no option

Take up the mantel and spread the word

Wake up, wake up.

My own voice echoes deep within

Outstretched fingers grasp remnants

From so far away arising occurs,

evasion is useless

Having sunk so low the journey is arduous.

Wake up, wake up.

Solitude - Delicious 2

Birdsong wakes me

At dawn darkness ebbs reluctantly

to reveal a coastal mist

Gray blanket that crept silently

in the night from the sea

Through valley and ford swirling

and twisting over vine

Cocooned in soft haze that floats

dull beyond my reach

Deer arcs a fence effortlessly

Prehistoric wild turkeys scuttling specter

like at the edge of dissipating fog

Gravel underfoot breaks the silence

and startles them gone

Heavy dew coats everything in a sticky gloss

Damp silence catches fresh

and crisp in my mouth

Warm plumes of breath

Thoughts need no voice,

words could never do sense justice

Moments of expression and experience

in this stumbled upon haven

Bleating lambs, feed bins and running

water amid skittish hooves

The day is brought to life as silence

slips away to rest

Solitude evaporates starkly

Chased by a barking dog and

children's call for breakfast.

I let it go, knowing that at sunset

I shall pick up my book again

The world will still in its natural cycle

here on this land

Naturally into transition and me along with it,

deliciously in awe.

Epiphany

It is not the dull edges of our lives

we need push against.

It is the seeking out of fresh sharp aspects

We have hidden away for safety sake

Expose them now as your very nature

Lean into them as inevitable if to live

Blood flowing freely,

Taste metallic on your tongue as you bite down

Savoring life

The secret to belief is having a reason to

Articulating emotion

Conveying feelings

In the context of disbelief concerning

Everything that is matters most.

Void

It's a peculiar thing to be outside of your family.

It's even more peculiar to have been placed

there against your wishes.

You spend all of your life nurturing

and protecting, because that is the job that you

took on when you decide to become

a husband and a father.

But to sit outside helplessly watching events

unfold and knowing that you have little

or no influence to help nurture and care

for the people you love

It is nothing short of abandonment.

It is a lonely place where you reap only

diminished influence and expanded

responsibilities for outcomes you have no part in.

Then you have to decide how to articulate

it without being stupid.

The question is, is it my opinion or perspective

that is unwanted, or simply,

The residue of years has worn everyone down to

Independence beyond their ken.

Elusive

Knocking gently,

you came to the door of my dream

Long dark winter coat and boots,

inviting me to walk

The scent of sweet rhubarb hung in your hair

Running from the rain as the hillside

path gently dipped

We found a covered bench and

sat close enough to touch

Hidden from view yet exposed in

our endeavor to connect

Time has a way of throwing distractions

on the path we share

Weighted responsibilities feigning

priority until our edges dull

Your outline harder to see,

your lips muted and words quiet

The moment spins like a fair ground

attraction as I hold tight

Memories and gut-wrenching feelings

flood me till dizzy

All I want is to hold you tight and

feel you within my reach

Stilted conversation on your sweet

breath as the rain falls

I watch your mouth, the questions

tumble out like butterflies

What is this, this delicate dance our

tired bodies remember

Let's stay here forever and reconstruct

the conversations past

Relive embraces and entangled moments

over miles and inches

Elbows touching lightly with more intensity than

torrid lovemaking

The rain stops when the sun breaks

out in dapple patches on hills

You shed your sodden coat to reveal

a spring dress and simple shoes

Light on your feet you step out from my

dream and I grasp desperately

You are a feeling that sits heavy upon

my chest now as I awake

I sniff the air of my dark bedroom hoping

for some lingering essence

Urgently reaching for paper to capture

you before you are gone forever.

Hector:
A Reflection of Sorts

In many ways, the intent of this book is about discovery of self, a tad indulgent but an honest reflection and shared journey. An arduous journey, yet when we embark, we find that life is full of all sorts of characters trying to figure out the meaning of life for themselves. Hector has much the same challenge as he considered venturing into the strange world outside his burrow. Even if we know where the answers lie, we always think that they are out there on some new and strange frontier, out where the grass is greener.

So, let's consider three things, *Time, Words*, and *Old dogs* or hedgehogs learning new tricks – Can we keep it that simple?

Time is the one thing we cannot acquire; we don't even know how much time we actually have in our lifetime. Regardless of wealth or stature, time is elusive. The best we can do is use it well. Make moments count by living fully in our element.

Words are a little more fun, there are plenty of them, and you can even make them up if you feel the need to. Words are how we describe our lives. Words articulate beliefs we have taken on over our lifetime without necessarily challenging or questioning their meaning. We seldom search for alternatives that are more apt to express our true selves. That is, of course, if you have broached the concept of "Me." Which brings us to the adage of "Old dogs or Hedgehogs, and new tricks".

You can't teach an old dog new tricks is the perfect idiom. Remember, an idiom is an expression that doesn't necessarily have a definition but more of an understanding behind it. How about – "It is never too late to learn". For some reason, we choose to "let a sleeping dog lie" as we perpetuate the vicious circle we have adopted on the journey from *Domestication*, through *Education*, into *Resignation*.

Perhaps we can discover some new frontiers. They are not that far away, and you can keep your slippers on or leap up in some yoga pants and shake off those ingrained beliefs.

What do we nurture? On what do we spend all that precious time?

o Growth and Spirituality

o Finances and Security

o Relationships and Family

o Health and Recreation

o Home and Work

o Creativity and Expression

How much time do you have?

Imagine our life was 24hrs and we could track the advance of time. What time it is in our life? Then we can figure out what to do with the time we have ahead of us rather than worry about the past that cannot be recovered.

When you were born, your 24-hour clock began ticking for the first time. According to the World Bank, life expectancy for an average human being currently numbers 78.4 years - 76 years for men and 81 years for women. The insurance industry, the banking industry, and the world of monetary standards have established actuarial tables that help them to govern the fiscal rules of life and death. So, if 78.4 years represents our average life span, we can assume our clock will hit 24 hours, or midnight when we reach that age. Some of us will live longer, some less.

We know that each of the 24 hours represents 3.267 years of life lived on our clock and that at 12:44 A.M, you are three years old. Likewise, three hours of living on the 24-hour clock is the same as three times 3.267 years of life, or 9.801 years. Therefore at 3 A.M., you will have lived almost ten years of life and begin your approach to adolescence.

When you reached the vibrant age of 20 years old, it is 6:24 A.M. in the morning. Most people are rising to get ready for work at that time. On our clock, you are rising to meet your life as a young adult, passionate, and full of promise.

At 9:18 A.M., you turn 30. Are you married, and do you have children by then? What does this morning mean to your emerging life pattern, have you begun to live in reason for gain vs passion for expression?

At 12:44 P.M. you turn 40, you are working in your third career? Were you married and already divorced? Your kids are almost ready to leave for college in the next few years? You start to wonder what happened to your passion?

As a person of 50 years old, you are looking at the clock, and it shows a time of 3:18 P.M. It is approaching dinnertime in your life. You have less than 9 hours of life remaining on the 24-hour clock. What will you do, what burns inside you calling out transition, what would it feel like to be in your element?

Another perspective might be.

A person of 60 years old is looking at the clock, and it shows a time of 6:22 P.M. They have less than 6 hours remaining on their 24-hour life clock. However, they have spent the past ten years present to their passion, creating equilibrium in their reasons for living. A sense of wellness embodies all that they do as they live in a state of grace. We applaud them for living fully. We admire and envy them for knowing the difference and taking the chance they have avoided the pursuit of Bigger, Better, Faster, More, asking what is enough?

Better still – Why stop and midnight?

3 P.M. is a beginning, not a demise. You do not have to die at midnight (78.4 years old) but go on and live the next chapter of your life in your element. The party only begins at midnight, 2am makes you almost 85 Years old. At 3am you are 88 years old and in the ranks of Charlie Chaplin and Geraldine 'Jerrie' Mock (89) who was the first woman to fly around the world solo when she was just 39. Then perhaps you will push all the way through to breakfast at 6am, you will be in the ranks of Louise Bourgeois the Influential Sculptor at 98 Years Young or

George Burns the entertainer who worked passionately up until the day he died at 100.

Outside of life and death, our personal 24-hour clock becomes another one of those unwanted absolutes. With that absolute comes the idea that we do not have very much time left to do what brings us alive or things that matter the most? What will those things be, and how will you make the most out of the adjustments you need to make? Now is an excellent time to begin that change, if you are not currently doing what matters the most. You better get started. Your 24-hour clock is ticking away.

Here are eight Hector inspired aspects of Creative Expression and living fully in your element where the grass is greenest.

1. Imagine	5. Reality
2. Crave	6. Essence
3. Create	7. Epiphany
4. Share	8. Element

Take some time and work through this list of aspects and questions. Consider how you might fashion a resolution of sorts that could be implemented in your own journey.

We all have a book of stories and ramblings, written or recited internally, seldom shared eternally, crafted with care and hidden away on some dusty shelf. Bring them into the light, share; you may be surprised by the results.

Have a little fun – start with your own initial Rambling like Hector, a spew of words that open the way to Creative Expression and a dropping of the guard or fear of vulnerability.

Leaping forward, consider something a little more expressive, don't wait 10 years like Hector, dive deeper. Call it what you will, a poem, a short story. Ignite the spark of Creative Expression as a catalyst to living fully in your element.

Oh! And share and see who is listening.

Imagine: *A possibility of sorts* –

"He could run, he could hide, he could survive like this, but he could not live like this."

Hector wonders how he got to this very now, how did he miss so much on the journey, he had lost the ability to see love and beauty in his world. The possibilities seem overwhelming in a life where change creates fear.

"Hector sat, not knowing what to do with the knowledge that everything he needed was here, right around him in plain sight."

A question of sorts:

What have you avoided in your life?

What is available to you?

A resolution of sorts:

_____

_____

_____

_____

_____

_____

Crave: *A desire of sorts* –

"Hector, or #7 for the time being, joined the wriggling pink fray in pursuit of the elusive teat."

Humble beginnings build character and tenacity it is said. It also creates the foundation of all our fears and perceived inadequacy at 4 or 5 years old we set a belief in place that encumbers us for a lifetime. How to untie that tangled knot of twisted threads we believe as true? We spend our lives trying to prove its truth.

"Life at ground level was where it started, and Hector was the recipient of that all too common prize that he now understood as mediocrity."

A question of sorts:

What sparks desire in you?

What beliefs prevent your expression?

A resolution of sorts:

_____

_____

_____

_____

_____

_____

Create: *An opportunity of sorts –*

"He wondered at the chances lost or gained between breaths, the opportunities missed or found in the blink of an eye and the sheer randomness of it all."

Hector explores the passion of youth and the internal gnaw that pushes out to explore his destiny. In taking that risk to explore beyond our natural habitat we discover the possibility of finding joy.

"The slightest leap, so small to the untrained eye, boundless and courageous to the fearful."

A question of sorts:

What chances have you missed?

What courageous leap can you make?

A resolution of sorts:

_____

_____

_____

_____

_____

_____

Share: *A necessity of sorts* –

"Hector felt himself suffocating again by the spectral no-thing, an immense mediocre shroud, draped in plain sight throughout his life, day after day."

Hiding in plain sight of those around us as we acquiesce to the demands of day-to-day life. It is a slow rot that eats at our soul if we are dishonest with others and ourselves as to our true passions, talents and desires. Our essence screams at us in dreams, in feelings and the eyes of our loved ones, we should listen.

"In this dream he had it all, wealth and fame. Yet the two simple things he truly wished for most had eluded him. Love and Joy."

A question of sorts:

What do you wish for?

Unconditionally what would you share?

A resolution of sorts:

_____

_____

_____

_____

_____

_____

Reality: *An awakening of sorts –*

"The day was warm, and Hector slid down to his belly and placed his snout on the ground, stopping for a moment."

Stop for a moment and look around, it is all here, everything you need or desire. Bigger, better, faster, more is the illusion we are indoctrinated into at birth. What has been the cost to self and others in the pursuit of the elusive fulfillment of superficial desires?

"I shall live unbound, for I have discovered that the grass is indeed greenest where I am."

A question of sorts:

What would you stop doing first?

Where is the grass greenest for you?

A resolution of sorts:

_____

_____

_____

_____

_____

_____

Essence: *A foundation of sorts* –

"I realized that I could have disappeared today, simply gone in an instant. Some may have wondered, I hope. Many would have just gone on with their day with the slightest ripple of me brushing against their memories. Then fading like a wisp of smoke upon the breeze, I would be gone forever."

It is in the simplest of things we discover our essence. Unguarded moments that reveal our true selves. It is also in our interactions with others we get to convey an expression of our humanity unchecked should we make ourselves vulnerable and available to play.

"The family had visited for the summer solstice and she had watched Hector teach the pups how to dunk for apples in the pond."

A question of sorts:

What is the essence of your life?

With whom and how would you play?

A resolution of sorts:

_____

_____

_____

_____

_____

_____

Epiphany: A revelation of sorts –

"Having one's slug and eating it was a desire he no longer pursued."

Emerging from the fog of perception and assumption the world becomes brighter. So much more seems possible without the encumbrance of fear and doubt. A lightness becomes us as we cast aside the overcoats of past insecurities and silly thinking. All is possible.

"Years pitted against his passion and now he had let it go, now free to explore the color that was always so close at hand yet hidden by his own grey perspective."

A question of sorts:

Can you define your epiphany?

What would "Unencumbered" feel like?

A resolution of sorts:

_____

_____

_____

_____

_____

_____

Element: A sharing of sorts –

"His passion had always been in writing, anything to let the mind wander. Boundless stories of imagining, life lived in a million different ways, so far from the limiting wanderings of fear."

Possibilities all wrapped up in the joy of sharing a delicious vulnerability, one's deepest thoughts, real or imagined.

Hiding behind our words, shrouding thoughts and feelings is a dis-ease. Opening up the pages, becoming vulnerable to self is the first step in relief.

"Hillary closed and kissed the little book; she tucked it into the side of the big leather chair where Hector would find it when he awoke.

A question of sorts:

What are you passionate about?

Who supports you in your creativity?

A revelation of sorts:

_____

_____

_____

_____

_____

_____

Expression: A creativity of sorts –

"The old and new ramblings expanded out into a simple form of poetry that Hector would not give a name to."

Our true Creative Expression can surprise us. Until we give it expression it holds no shape or form, or even power if it is to inspire. In revelation and expression, it brings us full circle back to our essential self, the greatest gift to embrace wholeheartedness.

"They would share his words together on still summer nights at the burrow entrance where years before they had discovered one another."

A question of sorts:

What is a wholehearted future?

To whom would you express it?

A resolution of sorts:

_____

_____

_____

_____

_____

_____

Your First Rambling: Free think an expression that pushes from your chest. Trust the words that spew out – nothing can be wrong.

_____

_____
_____
_____
_____
_____
_____
_____
_____
_____
_____
_____
_____
_____
_____
_____
_____
_____
_____
_____
_____
_____

I can share this with -

Inspirational words to draw from:

ARTISTIC / ACTIVE / ASTONISHING / AFFECTIONATE / ACCOMPLISHED / ANCHORED / ADORED / BOLD / BRAVE / BOUNTIFUL / DETERMINED / DYNAMIC / EXCITED / EARNEST / ECSTATIC / ENLIGHTEND / EXCITED / ELEQUENT / FESTIVE / FORTUNATE / FEARLESS / FORTHRIGHT / GENEROUS / GRACEFUL / GROUNDED / GROWING / HARMONIOUS / HEARTFELT / HILARIOUS / HONOURABLE / INQUISITIVE / INSPIRED/ IMPORTANT / IMPECABLE / INTENTIONAL / ILLUSTRIOUS / IMPRESSIVE / JUBILANT / JOYOUS / JUBILANT / KINDRED / KNOWLEDGEABLE / KINDHEARTED / LOYALTY / LEGITIMATE / LUMINOUS / MAGNIFICENT / MAJESTIC / MEMORABLE / MONUMENTAL / MORAL / MYSTERIOUS / NOTEWORTHY / NUTRITIOUS / NATURAL / OPTIMAL / ORIGIONAL / ORCHESTRATE / OFFICIAL / PASSIONATE / POSITIVE/POWERFULL/PRECIOUS/PRODUCTIVE / QUINTISENTIAL / QUALIFIED / RADIANT / REMARKABLE / RESPECTFUL / ROWDY / SERENE / STUPENDOUS / SENTIMENTAL / SHAMELESS / SPECTACULAR / STIMULATING / SUBSTANTIAL / SUPPORTIVE / TERRIFIC / THUNDEROUS / TREASURED / TRUSTWORTHY / UNFOLD / VALUABLE / VIVACIOUS / WHOLEHEARTED / WORTHWHILE /

Build your own lists to inspire & reference

Your First Poem: Wait a while – a week, a month or two after the Ramble. Then, take a deep breath, slowly release your breath as the words reveal themselves to you – Trust your Essence.

_____

_____

_____

_____

_____

_____

_____

_____

_____

_____

_____

_____

_____

_____

_____

_____

_____

_____

_____

I can share this with –

Vulnerability: An epiphany of sorts

Writing "Hector" was not about writing, it was an exercise in cracking open the mold I had cast myself into for the past 45 years. A finely crafted facade of everything I believed that I stood for. I had been telling stories for years, and I believed all of them.

Growing up I learned never to be vulnerable, taught to guard my most personal feelings, aspirations, and weaknesses. There was always the threat of attack, ridicule, often by the ones closest to me.

At my first book reading, I realized too late that I had dropped my well-formed guard. I had crafted a story to hide behind a Hedgehog; I should have chosen something bigger! My voice broke, and I ran straight into vulnerability, tears welled, and I had nowhere to run, I read on and learned that respect meets vulnerability in an overlap of grace. A state of grace, I had never felt it was my element, and the room was full of people who understood it perfectly.

Once open and exposed change became inevitable, I had imagined it in fear; I now craved it in reality. For the past few years, I have been creating my element, exploring higher levels of grace, honing my newfound vulnerability. I have been empowered by distilling my sense of value in this new landscape. It has been with the help of so many gentle and giving souls who believe in living wholeheartedly. Many woke up long before 3 P.M. and have taken their time to guide and mentor me.

They evoked my desire to share my own path, my 3 P.M., a simple process of evoking and defining the elements of my life and the return I desired. Evoke is a way to explore and learn how to balance between Reason and Passion, how to listen to the applause of your own creativity and resplendent wholeheartedness.

Evoke: A method of sorts

Most of us struggle to balance between Passion and Reason, Vision, and Action. The EVOKE method provides a simple process to establish the guide rails within which to build a toolbox of skills and a roadmap to guide you on the journey of transformation to the desired destination or expression you envision for yourself. The goal is not just to be in balance, but to learn how to find equilibrium when in the constant "state of flux" that is life on an ongoing basis. Many initiatives will evolve out of the EVOKE process, each unique to your vision or particular to you as the one driving the transition. The clarity of objective ensures that the right initiatives will emerge.

What will you be if you change – you will be different!

You will discover something very absolute about yourself in this exercise.

This type of process requires you to make some severe adjustments in your life. You begin to work on developing the things you can do that are the most important things you should be doing. This is *Self-epiphany* rather than *Self-help*.

We call this process EVOKE for a few reasons, a methodology to prompt a transition from the safety of reason to the risk of passion and possibilities, wellness through creativity, and the realization of your natural state, being in your element...

3 P.M. = *Purpose, People, Place,* and *Message* to achieve the *Return (R.O.I. return on investment)* you desire. You eliminate things that do not matter as much and begin to focus on the ones that matter the most. Regardless of age or time remaining, we can begin to work on developing the expression of our essence instead of what keeps the status quo.

Your clock is too short to permit useless activities to steal your precious time and the sharing of your gifts.

Ask yourself five simple questions and begin the journey so many avoid.

PURPOSE: Are you creating a life you want, need, or desire?

PEOPLE: Are you engaging with the right people to achieve that life?

PLACE: Have you created a physical reality of the life you imagine?

MESSAGE: Are you keeping or fulfilling the promises you make to yourself?

RETURN: What is your life worth to you, and are you rewarded?

W.B. Yeats once wrote:

"It takes more courage to examine the dark corners of your own soul than it does for a soldier to fight on a battlefield."

Find one word only for each answer and craft an "Essence Statement." It is the seed of expression.

Here are my Personal and Professional Essence Statements:

PURPOSE: Imagine

PEOPLE: Crave

PLACE: Create

MESSAGE: Share

RETURN: Expression

Personal – *Essence*

*"I live fully by taking time to discover my true **expression** beyond simple reason. Through **creativity** I nurture my **imagination** to reveal my intrinsic passion. I **crave** the action of individuals who desire to shift paradigms, and*

who aspire to **share** as masters of their particular craft and live fully in their element."

Broken Down – DNA (Why – What – How)

Why – *Discover*
I live fully by taking time to discover my true **expression** beyond simple reason.

What – *Nurture*
Through **creativity** I nurture my **imagination** to reveal my intrinsic passion.

How – *Act*
I **crave** the interaction of individuals who desire to shift paradigms, and who aspire to **share** as masters of their particular craft and live fully in their element.

Professional – *Essence*
The aspects of EVOKE are explored by individuals who desire to shift paradigms, and who aspire to be masters of their particular craft and live fully in their element.

E – Expertise: What you are really good at.

V – Vulnerable: How you openly share expertise.

O – Orchestrate: What platform you need to share.

K – Knowledge: How you convey core knowledge.

E – Expression: What you do in your element.

The aim is to create new methods of distilling ideas that evoke thought, from Reason to Passion and back again. EVOKE works to establish a unique definition of one's, *Purpose, People, Place, Message*, (3 P.M.), and desired *Return*. This process has been established and practiced over time, personally and professionally, when creating wholehearted, actionable, roadmaps to reveal your essence so as to live fully in your element.

I look forward to meeting you

Visit us at www. GaryFinnan.com

Author and Artists

Gary Finnan was born in Scotland and raised in Zimbabwe and South Africa.

Gary splits his time with his wife and two daughters between California and South Carolina. Gary is an award-winning author and sought-after designer, speaker, and Creative Expression coach.

Camryn Finnan was born in South Africa and is an animal advocate. When she was in 8th grade Camryn read several pages of Hector and proceeded to offer up some of her drawings after hearing that the book needed an illustrator. Camryn wants to train anti-poaching dogs and return to Africa.

Elina Cherianidou – Illustrator Artist – Elina was born in Viborg near St. Petersburg in Russia. She is an architect and children book illustrator. Elina lives with her family in Greece. The hedgehogs have always been one of her favorite animals.

www.ingramcontent.com/pod-product-compliance
Lightning Source LLC
Chambersburg PA
CBHW020249130626
46549CB00005B/2131

9 7 9 8 9 8 7 6 0 1 5 1 8